21st Century Skills INNOVATION Library

Disease Control

by Susan H. Gray

Published in the United States of America by Cherry Lake Publishing
Ann Arbor, Michigan
www.cherrylakepublishing.com

Content Adviser: Noshene Ranjbar, MD

Design: The Design Lab

Photo Credits: Cover and page 3, ©Pedro Nogueira, used under license from Shutterstock,
Inc.; page 4, ©iStockphoto.com/Funwithfood; page 6, ©iStockphoto.com/nico_blue; page 8,
©Visual Arts Library (London)/Alamy; page 11, ©Classic Image/Alamy; page 13, ©AP Photo;
page 16, ©Charles O. Cecil/Alamy; page 17, ©matthias stolt/Alamy; page 19, ©Greenshoots
Communications/Alamy; page 21, ©Picture Contact/Alamy; page 23, ©Terry Whittaker/Alamy;
page 25, ©qaphotos.com/Alamy; page 27, ©AP Photo/Rene Macura; page 28, ©Marc Dietrich,
used under license from Shutterstock, Inc.

Library of Congress Cataloging-in-Publication Data
Gray, Susan Heinrichs.
  Disease control / by Susan H. Gray.
    p. cm. —(Innovation in medicine)
  Includes index.
  ISBN-13: 978-1-60279-228-9
  ISBN-10: 1-60279-228-3
  1. Epidemiology—Juvenile literature. I. Title. II. Series.
  RA653.5.G72 2009
  614.4—dc22   2008004354

*Cherry Lake Publishing would like to acknowledge the work of
The Partnership for 21st Century Skills.
Please visit www.21stcenturyskills.org for more information.*

CONTENTS

Chapter One
Wind, Water, and Spirits   4

Chapter Two
Many People with Many Talents 10

Chapter Three
Even More Tools   16

Chapter Four
What's in the Future?   19

Chapter Five
Changing Minds   22

Glossary   30
For More Information   31
Index   32
About the Author   32

Wind, Water, and Spirits

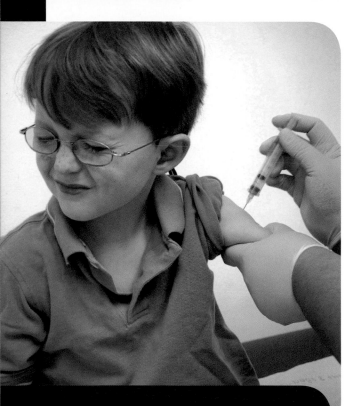

Before they can enter school, most children have to be vaccinated against a number of diseases.

"Ouch!" whimpered Brandon as Dr. Devi gave him a shot.

"It'll be okay," Alex told his little brother. "It won't hurt for long. And this will help you not get sick. Right, Dr. Devi?"

"Absolutely," the doctor told Alex. "And you should feel lucky," she continued, turning to Brandon. "That little pinch was a **vaccine**. And getting that injection is a lot easier than fighting some of the diseases people used to get."

"Like what?" both boys asked at once.

And the doctor started to explain.

❖ ❖ ❖

Human beings have always wondered what causes disease. To answer that, doctors through the ages have come up with all sorts of ideas. They have also thought of interesting ways to avoid diseases and to keep them under control.

A Greek doctor named Hippocrates wrote of disease 2,400 years ago. Some illnesses, he wrote, had to do with wind, water, and the seasons. Hippocrates warned people who were traveling to new cities. He advised them to check on the quality of the city's wind and water. He thought that was one way to avoid disease.

For centuries, the causes of diseases remained a mystery. Different cultures had their "experts" to explain things. Some blamed evil spirits when people got sick. Others said "bad air" was at fault. No one had any proof for such beliefs. Worse still, no one was seriously looking for the real causes.

In the early 1500s, the Italian doctor Girolamo Fracastoro began studying disease. He believed that many illnesses were caused by tiny beings that could somehow multiply themselves. He also thought that they could pass from one person to the next. Fracastoro was far ahead of his time. It would be many years before his ideas were shown to be true.

Eventually, scientists began to realize they needed better ways to think about disease. Otherwise they had no hope of predicting when a disease might appear—and they'd never learn how to stop it. Blaming evil spirits and bad air would no longer do.

Scientists saw that they needed to gather information on each disease they came across. They needed to look at many patients to figure out what caused the disease. They also needed to interview their patients and to look at

Centuries ago, Bernardino Ramazzini began to ask patients questions to learn more about their illnesses. Today, doctors follow this practice by talking to patients about what they eat, what medicines they take, and what sicknesses their family members have had.

their **environments**. In some cases, they might need to look at the entire population of a place. They may have to follow the spread of a disease over time, too.

Bernardino Ramazzini helped foster this way of thinking in Italy. In 1700, he wrote out instructions for doctors. He told them to ask their patients many questions. He said they should ask their patients where they worked. Ramazzini thought that some diseases were related to certain jobs.

The 19th century had several innovators. In 1838, William Farr started a new system in Great Britain to record deaths. Earlier systems often reported only that a person had died "suddenly." Farr wanted more information than that. He wanted the cause of death to be recorded.

Farr didn't stop there. He knew that doctors throughout Great Britain used different names for the same diseases. No one seemed to agree on who died of what. So Farr created a system for classifying illnesses. He asked doctors to send him information on different diseases, the names of the diseases, and also the nicknames that people had given them. Their responses helped him to organize a list of 27 fatal diseases, along with very specific descriptions. Whenever a person died, the local physician was to look at the list and write down the exact cause of death.

Another person interested in disease was Dr. John Snow. He lived in England during terrible **cholera epidemics** that raged between 1831 and 1854. He looked at how cholera spread, what parts of his town were hit the worst, and which areas seemed to be safe.

Louis Pasteur's medical experiments gave doctors a new understanding of how germs work and how to avoid them.

He made maps of neighborhoods showing where the disease was most common. Dr. Snow was tireless. He was also very organized and paid attention to details. He figured out the cause of the epidemics and spread the word through his writings.

Throughout Europe, other scientists were looking at disease in new ways. For example, Louis Pasteur of France found that germs could cause disease. Robert Koch of Germany made guidelines to help scientists figure out exactly which germs caused which diseases.

Many scientists were studying diseases—how they develop and how they could be controlled. These people interviewed patients, studied germs, took careful notes, and noticed patterns. They didn't realize it, but they were building the foundation for a field of medical science known as **epidemiology**.

Life & Career Skills

The word *epidemiology* comes from Greek words meaning "the study of what is upon the people." Epidemiologists do not focus on how a certain disease affects a sick person. They study how diseases affect entire populations, or groups of people. They look at how and why diseases spread. They figure out how people can avoid getting them. Then they explain things to other scientists. They also share the information with the public.

CHAPTER TWO

Many People with Many Talents

Epidemiologists come from many different fields. Some are interested in math. They find out how many people have a certain disease, where they live and work, and other details. They sort through their data and try to find patterns. Once they find a pattern, they can sometimes predict how and where the disease will spread.

Other epidemiologists like to teach. They are good at explaining diseases to people. They teach doctors or nurses about a disease that is spreading. They also write articles telling the public how to protect themselves against diseases.

Many epidemiologists are interested in science and medicine. Over the last 100 years, there have been a number of innovations in these fields. Some innovations were inspired by the work of Edward Jenner.

Before Dr. Edward Jenner and his smallpox vaccine, getting smallpox meant almost certain death.

Jenner was an English doctor. He knew that cows got a disease called cowpox and humans got a similar disease called smallpox. In Jenner's day, smallpox killed thousands of people. He knew that people who milked sick cows got cowpox blisters but never seemed to get smallpox. Jenner wondered if contact with infected cows strengthened people against smallpox. In 1796, he tried a daring experiment.

He took fluid from a milkmaid's cowpox blister and injected it into a young boy. He did this for several days, slowly increasing the dose. Then he deliberately injected the boy with the smallpox germ. The boy got sick, then recovered completely. Jenner found that the human body could strengthen itself against a disease. But it first needed to experience weak contact with the disease. The contact came as a mild injection of germs. This type of injection is now called a vaccine. At first, scientists rejected Jenner's discovery. But eventually, they saw that it worked.

Smallpox was just one disease, though. Could there be vaccines for other diseases? Many scientists in the 20th century thought so. After years of hard work, they created vaccines for the flu, polio, rabies, and many other diseases.

Developing a vaccine is not easy, and scientists run into many problems. The polio vaccine is one such example.

The muscles of polio victims become weak. Some people become **paralyzed**, and others even die. Dr. Jonas Salk of the United States wanted to help these people. He began working on a vaccine. After several years, his vaccine was ready to use. Thousands of children across the United States received it. Soon the number of new polio cases began dropping. Then something happened.

Suddenly, about 200 people who got the vaccine also got the disease, and 11 died. What went wrong? Were

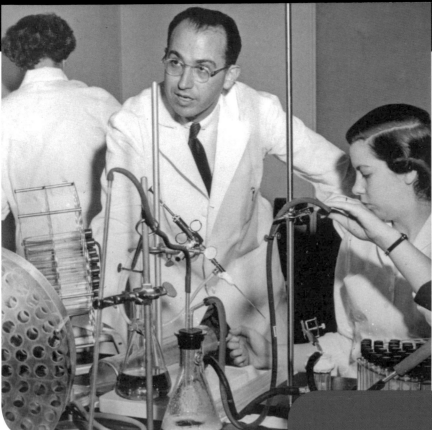

Dr. Jonas E. Salk played a key role in fighting polio.

there bad batches of vaccine? Were the vaccines stored in poor containers? Were doctors and nurses injecting people incorrectly? Scientists began to investigate.

As it turned out, one company had produced a poorly made batch. It had caused the disease instead of preventing it. Scientists came up with new rules for vaccine production, and injections resumed. In the United States, new cases almost disappeared.

Using vaccines is one of the ways to prevent disease, because vaccines make people's **immune systems** stronger against outside germs. But vaccines can be

Learning & Innovation Skills

 In 1946, the United States government opened a new office called the Communicable Disease Center, or CDC. Its main goal was to fight malaria—a disease spread by mosquito bites. Malaria causes fever, chills, muscle aches, and even death. The CDC's job was to find enough tank trucks and insect spray to kill mosquitoes in the southeastern United States.

Since those early years, the CDC has taken on more and more public health issues. It now has many experts who gather disease information and who teach people how to avoid illness. It has also changed its name to the Centers for Disease Control and Prevention. Although malaria is no longer a big problem in the United States, CDC workers still study it. They share their information with people in countries where the disease continues to spread.

expensive to make. Another way to improve the health of a population is to address the **symptoms** that a disease produces. For instance, one symptom of some fatal infections is **dehydration** from diarrhea. To treat this, doctors use a simple, lifesaving solution called ORS.

ORS is short for **oral rehydration** solution. It is a mixture of water, sugar, and salt. It was developed in the 1960s to keep people from dying of diarrhea. Diarrhea is not a disease, but it is a symptom of many diseases and can help illness to spread. It also causes millions of deaths each year, especially in children.

Before ORS, doctors knew that they could save these children—but only if they came to hospitals. Two scientists, Richard Cash and David Nalin, thought this was ridiculous. Cash and Nalin worked in Bangladesh, a very poor country. They developed a simple, easy-to-make drink of clean water, sugar, and salt. It kept people alive, even those with the worst diarrhea. Surely, the two scientists thought, everyone would want this mixture.

But they were wrong. Doctors in Bangladesh still wanted people to come to the hospital. Many mothers could not read the instructions to make the drink for their children. Roads were poor, so it was difficult to get salt and sugar packets out to the villages. How could Cash and Nalin solve these problems?

They turned to the people themselves. With help, they taught thousands of women how to make the solution. Those women went out to the countryside and villages. They taught other women how to make it. Schoolteachers also learned to mix the drink, and they taught children. The word spread, and things began to turn around.

Cash and Nalin's mixture is now used in many countries. It is a cheap, simple lifesaver. Thanks to its use, childhood deaths from diarrhea have dropped by more than half.

CHAPTER THREE

Even More Tools

The World Health Organization is helping to educate people in many countries about diseases that may affect them.

Cash and Nalin counted on women to walk the dirt roads and spread the news about ORS. This was a very low-tech way to stop the spread of disease, but it was the best way in Bangladesh. In other countries, people have used computers and the Internet to help control disease.

The World Health Organization (WHO) was started in 1948 to help improve the

Doctors all over the world use materials from the World Health Organization to learn about diseases and new treatments.

health of people all over the world. The organization has experts who study everything from cancer to food safety to disease outbreaks. They work to spread health information to the public.

Over the years, more and more information poured in to the WHO about diseases in different countries. Workers wondered how to keep track of all the data. Could computers help?

By using different computer programs, health experts found they could quickly look at disease data from all over the world. They could see where certain diseases

21st Century Content

At one time, leprosy was common in many countries. Also called Hansen's disease, it is spread from person to person by a kind of germ. The disease damages the skin, nerves, hands, feet, and eyes. In some countries, people with leprosy are ashamed of their disease. They are forced to live separately from the rest of society.

Certain drugs can cure leprosy. Since 1995, the World Health Organization has offered these drugs for free to anyone in the world who needs them. Though the number of new leprosy cases has dropped, thousands of new cases arise every year. Why do you think this still happens? Why doesn't everyone get these free drugs?

were growing and where others were disappearing. They could create maps and watch how diseases spread from week to week. They could even predict where a disease might show up next.

WHO experts began using e-mail and the Internet. They now use these tools to collect information from many countries. They also use them to warn people about diseases that are spreading and to explain the best protection.

The WHO is not the only group using such tools. State health departments all over America and health organizations in other countries use them to track diseases.

CHAPTER FOUR

What's in the Future?

It is never easy to keep a disease from spreading. People must be able to recognize diseases and report them. Experts must compare reports from different places to see if a disease is spreading. Doctors must obtain the medicines needed to treat it. The public must learn how to avoid the disease. Much of the future work in epidemiology has to do with speeding up and improving these activities.

Many organizations help educate the public about disease prevention. Some have clinics that offer vaccination.

21st Century Content

 In recent years, the World Health Organization has been watching out for bird flu, a disease caused by a virus that is carried by birds. WHO scientists track down and record all the cases of this flu in different countries. Then they make maps showing where those cases are.

From time to time, they look at the changes in the maps. Why do they do this? What does it tell them about the bird flu?

In many countries today, health care workers are learning to teach people about disease. They are learning ways to teach people who cannot read, who live far away from hospitals, or who still believe that evil forces cause disease. As these workers go into more and more remote areas, they will need to learn the best ways to teach the people they meet.

As travel between countries increases, the chances for disease to spread also increase. This means that scientists and computer experts will need to find ways to gather and interpret disease data more quickly. They will need to find speedier methods to warn people about the spreading disease.

Scientists are working to develop new vaccines. These might protect people against germs that attack the brain, lungs, and other organs. Chemists will work on ways to produce these vaccines quickly and cheaply.

In addition, many health care workers specialize in a growing field called holistic medicine or complementary and alternative medicine. This approach looks at the

African villagers wait in line outside a tent where free vaccinations are being administered.

health of a person as a whole. Then doctors suggest ways to improve the body's immune system and to fight germs and diseases naturally.

CHAPTER FIVE

Changing Minds

In the history of epidemiology, the greatest innovators were people who had new ideas and put them to the test. This was never easy for them. They had to work against what everyone else thought.

Giovanni Maria Lancisi

Giovanni Maria Lancisi of Rome was one innovator who worked to change the way people thought about disease. Lancisi was born in 1654, and even as a young boy, he showed an interest in science. When he was 18, he completed his studies to become a doctor. Lancisi was a very gifted and observant scientist. He wrote about various diseases including malaria. At the time, everyone thought that breathing "bad air" caused people to get the disease. In fact, the word *malaria* comes from the Italian words for "bad air."

This child in Vietnam sleeps under a mosquito net, which protects her from the insects. Giovanni Maria Lancisi discovered that mosquitoes spread malaria, a disease that people still suffer from today.

Lancisi noticed that people with malaria usually lived near swamps or marshy areas. He believed that the mosquitoes in these areas were the cause of the disease. He even said that swamps should be drained to keep malaria from spreading. Lancisi refused to believe that bad air caused the disease. His thinking was far ahead of his time. About 180 years later, scientists discovered exactly how mosquitoes spread the disease. They realized that Lancisi had been right all along.

John Snow

John Snow lived in England in the 1800s. At 14, he began studying medicine with a local doctor. Four years later, he saw his first cholera epidemic. Cholera victims experience diarrhea and vomiting so severe that they die from the loss of fluids. People in Snow's time had no idea what caused the disease. Worse, no one was seriously investigating it. They blamed it on everything from breathing polluted air to drinking beer.

Snow went on to become a doctor. And when he was 35, a second epidemic hit. As he treated his patients, he noticed they complained only of digestive problems. They did not have pain in their noses, throats, or lungs. This told him that polluted air was not the problem; it was something his patients ate or drank. Snow even thought that some extremely small **organism** might cause the disease. And perhaps the organism spread through the sewers and water systems in infected neighborhoods. Other doctors rejected his ideas. Snow had no proof, they said—and besides, everyone knew that polluted air was the problem.

A water education officer shows South African villagers how to test their local water. The work of Dr. John Snow helped medical researchers understand that disease can be spread through the water supply.

In August 1854, a third epidemic hit, this time in the London district where Snow worked. Snow tracked down the district's water supply. He found two supply companies and both drew water from the river that flowed through town. One company drew water from an area polluted by sewage. The other drew from a clean area upstream. Snow then visited homes throughout the district. He found out which water companies supplied which homes. He also learned which homes had cholera deaths. The more information he gathered, the more excited he became. The polluted water company supplied 286 of the victims, while the clean one supplied only 14 of them! Surely, he thought, the experts could see this connection.

But again, they were not impressed. A few weeks later, another outbreak occurred, and Snow found the address of each victim. He drew up a map and marked each address. He found out which public water pump all of the victims used. He was sure its water was polluted. Snow took his numbers and his map to the Board of Health. He asked them to remove the handle from the pump so that no one could use it. The board agreed, and immediately the outbreak ended. In the end, the experts' slow acceptance of Dr. Snow's ideas cost tens of thousands of lives.

Richard Doll

Dr. Richard Doll was an innovative thinker of the 20th century. He is best known for his work on tobacco smoking. At one time, smoking was thought to be harmless. Some people even believed that smoking could improve their health.

Dr. Richard Doll is applauded as he receives an award in 2003. He discoverd a link between cigarette smoking and lung cancer.

But early in the 20th century, doctors noticed that deaths from lung cancer were going up. Doll began to look into it. At first, he thought that fresh road tar was the problem. He believed that people who breathed its fumes got cancer. But then he began interviewing lung cancer patients. Soon the facts became clear. Smoking was to blame.

Doll wrote about what he had discovered, but he was ignored. Nonetheless, he continued to gather information

Thanks to the efforts of Dr. Richard Doll, the public now knows that cigarette smoking leads to cancer and other diseases. The best solution is to stop smoking—or never start.

and spread the word. Finally, people began paying attention. Over the next few years, he tirelessly worked to learn more about lung cancer. He collected information from thousands of smokers. He found that lung cancer was much more common in smokers than in nonsmokers. He discovered that people who quit smoking would decrease their chances of getting cancer. He also found that many other diseases were related to smoking. His efforts, and those of many more scientists and doctors, have saved the lives of thousands of people.

Life & Career Skills

The ideas of innovative thinkers, such as Dr. Richard Doll, are often ignored when they are first made public. Innovators must be able to keep working toward something they believe in even if others think they are wrong. They need good communication skills to be successful in getting others to change their minds and see the value in their work.

Glossary

cholera (KAH-luh-ruh) an often deadly disease in which people experience vomiting, diarrhea, and great loss of fluids

dehydration (dee-hye-DRAY-shuhn) the process of removing fluids from the body

environments (en-VYE-ruhn-muhnts) the places where people live and work

epidemics (eh-puh-DEH-miks) outbreaks of disease that affect a large number of people in the same area at the same time

epidemiology (eh-puh-dee-mee-AH-luh-jee) the study of the detection and spread of disease in large populations

immune systems (ih-MYOON SISS-tuhmz) the mechanisms by which the body protects itself from disease

oral (OR-uhl) having to do with the mouth; taken through the mouth

organism (OR-guh-niz-uhm) a living thing

paralyzed (PA-ruh-lyzd) unable to move or feel part of the body, such as the legs or arms

rehydration (ree-hy-DRAY-shuhn) having to do with restoring fluid to someone or something

symptoms (SIMP-tuhmz) signs of something

vaccine (vak-SEEN) a drug given to people to keep them from getting a particular disease

For More Information

BOOKS

Alphin, Elaine Marie. *Germ Hunter: A Story about Louis Pasteur*. Minneapolis: Carolrhoda Books, 2003.

Barnard, Bryn. *Outbreak! Plagues That Changed History*. New York: Crown Publishers, 2005.

Elliott, Lynne. *Medieval Medicine and the Plague*. New York: Crabtree Publishing, 2006.

Rodriguez, Ana Maria. *Edward Jenner: Conqueror of Smallpox*. Berkeley Heights, NJ: Enslow Publishers, 2006.

WEB SITES

Centers for Disease Control and Prevention: Rabies Web Page for Kids
www.cdc.gov/ncidod/dvrd/kidsrabies
A kids' Web site about rabies, its vaccine, and how the disease spreads

Healthfinder: Kids
www.healthfinder.gov/kids
Health games and information for kids

National Institute of Environmental Health Sciences
kids.niehs.nih.gov/epidemiology.htm
Learn more about epidemiology and other careers in science and health care

Index

alternative medicine.
    See holistic medicine.

bird flu, 20

Cash, Richard, 14–15,
    16
Centers for Disease
    Control and
    Prevention (CDC), 14
cholera, 8–9, 24–26
classification system, 7
Communicable Disease
    Center (CDC), 14
communication, 29
complementary
    medicine. *See* holistic
    medicine.
computers, 16, 17–18,
    20
cowpox, 11, 12

data, 10, 17, 20
diarrhea, 14, 15, 24
Doll, Richard, 26–29

education, 15, 17, 20
e-mail, 18
epidemics, 8–9, 24, 25
epidemiology, 9, 10,
    19, 22

Farr, William, 7
Fracastoro, Girolamo, 5

germs, 9, 12, 13, 18,
    20, 21

Hansen's disease. *See*
    leprosy.
Hippocrates (Greek
    doctor), 5
history, 5–9
holistic medicine,
    20–21

immune system, 13, 21
Internet, 16, 18

Jenner, Edward, 10–12

Koch, Robert, 9

Lancisi, Giovanni Maria,
    22–24
leprosy, 18
lung cancer, 27–29

malaria, 14, 22–24
mosquitoes, 14, 23, 24

Nalin, David, 14–15, 16

ORS (oral rehydration
    solution), 14–15, 16
outbreaks, 17, 26

Pasteur, Louis, 9
patterns, 9, 10

polio, 12–13

Ramazzini, Bernardino,
    7
remote areas, 14–15,
    20

safety, 13, 17
Salk, Jonas, 12
smallpox, 11, 12
smoking, 26–29
Snow, John, 8–9,
    24–26
symptoms, 14

vaccines, 4, 12–14, 20

World Health
    Organization (WHO),
    16–17, 18, 20

About the Author

Susan H. Gray has a master's degree in zoology. She has taught college-level courses in biology, anatomy, and physiology. She also has written more than 90 science and reference books for children. In her free time, she likes to garden and play the piano. Susan lives in Cabot, Arkansas, with her husband, Michael, and many pets.